Let's Dance

Square Dancing

By Mark Thomas

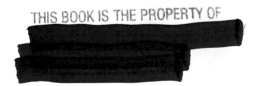

Children's Press
A Division of Grolier Publishing
New York / London / Hong Kong / Sydney
Danbury, Connecticut

Thanks to the students of the Delaware Valley Square and Round Dance Federation

Photo Credits: Cover and all photos by Maura Boruchow
Contributing Editor: Jeri Cipriano
Book Design: Christopher Logan

Visit Children's Press on the Internet at:
http://publishing.grolier.com

Library of Congress Cataloging-in-Publication Data

Thomas, Mark, 1963-
  Square dancing / by Mark Thomas.
   p. cm. — (Let's dance)
  Includes bibliographical references and index.
  ISBN 0-516-23145-6 (lib. bdg.) — ISBN 0-516-23070-0 (pbk.)
  1. Square dancing—Juvenile literature. [1. Square dancing.] I. Title.

 GV1763 .T56 2000
 793.3'4—dc21

                                                          00-034633

Contents

My name is Bobby.

I like square dancing with my friends.

5

We need eight people
to square-dance.

We each find a **partner**.

Partners stand to make
a square.

7

We dance to country music or **folk music**.

The music is fast.

Square dancing has a **caller**.

The caller tells us which **dance steps** to do.

11

The caller starts the square dance.

My partner and I step into the square.

13

Another **couple** meets us.

We touch hands with the other couple.

15

The caller stops us.

It is time to change places!

We step back and make the square again.

17

The caller calls another step.

All partners stand back to back.

Now partners dance around each other.

This step is the "**do-si-do**." (**doh**-see-**doh**)

We love square dancing!

21

New Words

caller (**caw**-ler) a person who calls out square dancing steps

couple (**kup**-l) two of kind

dance steps (**dans stehpz**) ways to move your feet and body to music

do-si-do (**doh**-see-**doh**) when partners dance back to back in a circle

folk music (**fohk myu**-zik) the music of a place or group of people

partner (**part**-ner) someone who dances with you

To Find Out More

Books
Basics of Square Dancing
by Pamela Morton
American Press

Square Dancing is for Me
by Mildred Hammond and James C. Tabb
Lerner Publications

Index

About the Author
Mark Thomas is a writer and educator who lives in Florida.

Reading Consultants

Kris Flynn, Coordinator, Small School District Literacy, The San Diego County Office of Education

Shelly Forys, Certified Reading Recovery Specialist, W.J. Zahnow Elementary School, Waterloo, IL

Peggy McNamara, Professor, Bank Street College of Education, Reading and Literacy Program